hinge

alycia pirmohamed

ignit**on**press

for Kaiden and Nikolai

First published in 2020
by **ignition**press
Oxford Brookes Poetry Centre
Oxford Brookes University
OX3 0BP

Cover design: Flora Hands, Carline Creative

A CIP record for this book is available from the British Library

ISBN 978-1-9161328-1-8

Contents

A map is a kind of short term memory: the genealogy of an historical time versus the chronology of geographical form.
Bhanu Kapil

My Body is a Forest

There is a face in the trees—

I lost a language
                     to the gap-toothed   birch.

Even the pine has learned how to swoon
when the wind
               deposits a secret.

A country is born knowing what it means
to waver.

A lost country is made by its daughters

and shame begins as a seed
                          that blossoms perennially
                     throughout generations.

Clove keeps the cha bitter—   for every dark cross

I apologise

          because I could not read the recipe
written in my grandmother's neat script.

I added cinnamon   crushed anise   mountain slope

          and too many quartered
Canadas—

once I watched a mule deer unfold her limbs
and vanish

               among the haloed trees

fog uncoiling at her heels   a ghost
inviting her

into its loosened borders.

In the blood of every migrant
        there is a map pointing home   this body

is an ode to the scattered landscapes
that have marbled my neck

with dark
hairs   and sharp   coarse

longings.
            Ask me how I remember her—

Not a face   but a movement

        legs stotting into a slip of boreal green.

A swatch of colour
        in the shape of a lost country.

A daughter   which is to say   an inherited vanishing

            through the slit of a dream.

Homeward

It began, you think, when your father buckled his seatbelt as instructed,
and the engine of the Boeing roared to life.

That was long ago, back when cigarette smoke clung
to the recycled cabin air, back when your father, who has since quit,

also stop-gapped the quadrants of his heart with fibres of ash and nicotine.
If you could place its beginning, the far-too-open

columns of your own heart, that slippery aortic eye of *missing something*,
it would be right there, in the seventies, when you were

not yet grassland seed, when your father chose a window seat
so that he might see the coastline as it receded—

and the emergence of that other coastline, a hinging spine of land that
hugged the s-shaped Atlantic Ocean,

its basin extending long, pleated arms toward him.
It was that coastline which mirrored not reflections, but the glittering face

of every single dream. Your father is where the act
of missing something first took root.

And although you have your grandmother's round face, and her double
moles across your forehead, those two small, dark comets,

you know it is from your father that you inherited this nebulous,
feeding sensation—this ever-increasing rift fashioning its distances
                                              within you.

In the heart of every migrant, there is a windrose pointing home
and while the needles within your own cells

flicker back and forth, your father is steadfast in direction:
homeward, a course you have only ever imagined, a flight path

you have learned may never exist for you—someone who stepped into
this world already in halves,

someone who dismantled Kutchi, allowing your first language to fall away
as you gathered English in your arms.

You never did quite fit into the stencil laid out for you:
your divisions being too long, too tall, too dark. *Too dark.*

Now, you place another gift in your suitcase: squares of chocolate
to bring barakat to those whom you have never met but

whose bloodlines trace back to the same tree.
Homeward, you think, as you zip closed your Western tongue,

along with t-shirts you will uncover and wear in this other country
you belong to, this country that was never content in your shadow,

and seeped through the borders of every new memory. Yes,
that was where it began, the fissuring, the splitting

of one stone into a multitude of loose ends:
with that first sweep across an ocean. And it makes sense

that it is him you will meet at the airport, your father, who will,
irrelevant of phenotype, look more like you than ever.

My Inheritance is to Long for [   ]

What knocks over the jar of cloves?
Each trembling spike

lands on the linoleum   scatters like the word for [   ].

My body is the shape of [   ] behind the grassland smoke.
I have my grandmother's silhouette

even with the backs of wild birch behind me—

if she is the ghost that unmakes
this second-generation belonging

hollowing my body into great-great-memory
splintering an ancestry

into a chasm

then I am the ghost in family photographs
a generation of crossings

becoming and unbecoming the country I long to know
its [   ] and whistling thorn.

I leave the window gaping like a lily's mouth
and welcome the   clatter

of fallen lines.
Her language slips and quivers between my teeth.

[   ] is the morning that clots itself like bloodlines
and the ache that unfurls

at the precipice of the throat—an unopened
dried flower bud

a woman's country
spilling into the room as if

to quell this need for wholeness

each branch the slender needle of a compass
      every corner an ode to my homeland.

Love Poem with Elk and Punctuation

To taste water
on the surface of a mirror—

to love, even briefly, the elk of your own tongue.

We become a myth that will cleave in the middle.
I admire spooling lotus after lotus after...

Fragment of my body:

brown edges, the whorl of a question mark
and you? Night's quiet whisper.

We become a bridge that crosses the chasm.

It takes a moon or two, a slivering, to chapter.
I look at the fringe

and watch evening kick her feet right through.

We, too, become hooves of light and feel our way
around tenderness—

this is a dream and we are the ruminants in it.

I want to know the ellipsoidal of you,
how you move

from polygon to speckle, rectangle to unravel.

In the water, I stretch out until I am lagoon
and you are the coral reef

at my toes,
until I am the lotus that blossoms after!

When the Wolves Appear

When the wolves appear, I know I am dreaming.
Give me back my dark.   They call out in Gujarati & no howling
could terrify me as much.   The wolf-eyes, like eyes in family photographs,
follow me.   I run & don't look back.
I am terrified of the land.   At sea, my body is a vase
filled with ovate black stones.   I sink
I sink   I sink.   Where have the wolves gone & where is the voice
that held the whorls of my fingers in its clay?
Is it fair to wish for them now? They don't belong in this version of a version
of India that wets my hair & deposits my skin onto the shore—
to get to the bone.   To get to the language.
I want to say *yes*   I want to become a stream of milk
& wash through the aquifers.   To pick up dark stalks of sugar along the way.
I want to carry my dark with me.   Stretch out legs of jasmine vine &
call out to the deep space between the stars.   Every night I open my mouth,
every night, my mouth is an orbiting, elliptical *no.*

Welcome

You know better than to feel welcome at anything resembling a border—
at least you do now, anyway

as you reckon anew with the forest ahead, dark cone after dark cone,
a hem of blue light signalling the horizon

as it peeks through the geometries. This drive will always, *always*,
remind you of childhood,

which, in turn, reminds you of nightfall and headlights in lieu of moons.
All of those times you sat in the front seat, two years shy

of the recommended age, watching the glow in front of you,
comfortably settled on one side of that other border,

that other hem—complicated and imperceptible—
wavering between a young girl and womanhood.

You realise it is the drive you remember,
with Vilna, Alberta as half-buck and half-headlight in memory.

Those few years, in which the world marked events in unison:
the turn into the new millennium, accompanied by an absolute fear

of how far we had travelled from zero,
and also, a different kind of distance, not to do with the vectors of time,

but the separation of one body from another,
the split into *they* and *us* once the towers fell. It is that one, even then,

young as you were, which has taught you the most lessons
about crossings. And everything you have written since that moment,

a moment which cut open every wound
you inherited, every wound you did not know you had,

is haunted by those extra spaces between lines,
your every impulse to add another gap,

another leap into some self you will never recall.
They and *us* coincided with rural thunderstorms and searching

for a stray tabby cat beneath the stammering pine
a cat, which your classmate had jabbed and kicked

for some unknown reason. This violence you will never understand—
at least, not beyond the way WELCOME edges further and further away

even as you walk right into your childhood eyes,
or the way "loss of innocence" does not, could not, really describe

how swiftly a country can turn its dial away from you.
This is where you curve east, toward Redwater,

and if the sun were out, there would be cattle alongside the road,
calves on their rickety legs, whole herds of glittering eyes

behind the fences. And on the other side, birch,
so much of it that you'd think,

in this case, a group of trees must also be called a herd
with their own rickety young stirring in the wind.

All of this you imagine as you glance in your rear-view mirror,
and somehow, you know this road is the line between it all:

what is named or what is nameless—
what is memory or what is seed.

Now, you look at the version of yourself that you have constructed,
a careful self-portrait, so precise in its languages that at times

she lives only in the penumbra of your words:
the young girl who counted out her *bismillahs* in the schoolyard each time

lightning embossed the field.
There is also that day, long before they fell, when you mixed egg yolks

in a friend's kitchen after a long walk from one trough to another.
There was peace then. An innate sort of harmony,

the kind you imagine must bring a cow to water.
The highway treads north, with Vilna now mounted on the road signs.

You can no longer tell if you are heading forward
or backward, save for the numbers ticking down.

Endearments

I have itemized
your   oak leaf   long limb   wild

& have begun to name you things like
"summer eclipse

in my offline calendar" or even "sleeping
under the stars

in a Wal-Mart parking lot"
& honestly

that kind of romance is okay with me
because secretly I have also named you "river of pine"

& "blossoming spring flower along the path to
Mount Yamnuska."

There is also my skin and yours,
there is also the way skin & skin are two

vastly different things
that this language has difficulty

capturing:
"every constellated mole" &

"pillar of shade."
How all of these names describe the way

we coexist
& exist within one another—

the way you disappear into the trees
& I follow.

Hinge

Tonight, I am all joint and animal dark. My heel blots out the moon,
    vanishes the small nod of light. And yes,
I prayed today, verging into my *bismillah* before settling
       on the broken.

I stoop into my longings, plot a seed in every corner. Last week,
    I titled another page with my body
and surrendered each bending, splitting line of myself
       to the making.

When we refer to plants, we call this positive phototropism,
         a body rivering toward the light.
I want to river toward the light, want to lean my neck toward
    a thing until I, too, become ism,

scientific and named into truth.
    Today, I walked through a dream that wasn't mine, and
thought of you waiting at the end of it,
       as if to gather me,

and maybe that's just the kind of woman I am—no matter
       how many times I halve the moon, or find myself in a room
without a window, I know Allah
         sees everything, every hand planting something new,

every metaphor for the tree it becomes. And, yes,
    I prayed today, but planting my palms together has never
felt like blossoming up the side of a mountain.
       The only time these hands have ever flowered,

have ever been used for something good,
        was that spring at Yamnuska, where we found a clear,
blue door of glacial water, and I walked right through
       your reflection.

Prairie Storm

We shoo away the hornet
as she lands on a grain of saffron rice.

Outside, the sky sparks like a wet nerve.
It must be lonely to be a storm,

long stems of water scattering sidelong
in a suddenly vacant wide.

The rain knows how to fall in Gujarati.
Afterward, bellies full

of clove heads and yolk, we spill
into the yard and read the dark rivers.

How quickly the landscape mothers
those stray tears,

bushels of mustard anchoring the roots
of an indivisible language.

And we marvel at how something
carried such a long distance

can fill the prairies like a vase,
as we, ourselves, pour and pour.

Self-addressed

Into the tall dark,
into the tamarack wood,
into a city, which at this hour
could be the shape
of any migrating bird.

This is me, driving straight
into my own life,
past the river frozen over
slick, the chokecherry's
saw-toothed edges—

into the roughage
of memories that surface slow
and tired, memories so like
the stars enacting
what is already gone.

I am grasping at
the things easiest to love:
Anas acuta, *Pinus resinosa*,
Anthaxia inornata, the
language of the prairies,

diction that I have held
like a dog with birch in her
mouth, a landscape that runs
through a body,
is a body—

into the boiling ginger,
into the neck of a loved one
folded like a leveret,
folded like a letter
     I wish you were here,
       I wish you were here—

How to Say Dark

There is a young girl at the riverbank,
knees and hair wet.

Her body unhinges like a black bear's mouth.
The salmon blink through

her every *Ya Allah*. There is no right answer
for how to feel peace.

She drifts in the water, a blur of girlhood
split too many times,

the ligament between korosho trees
and lodgepole pine. To a young daughter

in a teeming body of water, it is a shame
that nothing below the meniscus

has a name but her—
so she calls one fish *plum* for its bruised

brown colour. She names the wet ferns
ripple as they scatter around her thighs.

Even the water in evening churns differently
from daylight green.

It darkens, and she knows better than most
how to say dark.

Elsewhere

She did not know the shape of
this country—   wide   darkjagged

bend in the river,
rock elm withering

into unfamiliar dark, needled forest.
She searched for water and the water

was a heartache tongued by wild deer.

In northern Alberta, she was a line of crow
edging into the unknown boreal,

a woman caught between remnants of a dream
and long mouths of birch.

Even the key of her body—
      jaggedlong   gentledark—

could not unlock this landscape.

Sometimes there is a fog thick enough
to hide the trees

and she imagines this country unwithers,
becomes a different land,

where her body is shaped like the river
and the river

shaped like belonging.

Elegy with Two Elk and a Compass

In Jasper, Alberta, I pass through the widowed poplars.
Evening hikes up its dark hems, trees begin howling their elegies,
when loosened from the thicket, two elk walk into my gaze.

Here, in the gap between needle point and destination,
there is an unkind earth that persists even as loss petals down
leaving the poplars bare. Earlier that day, I had crossed
the forest's bridges and stepped beyond its corridors.

I had longed to find the hidden trail that led to the valley of roses.

From the elk, I am expecting a lesson, as if Allah has approached me
in the shape of a compass built from antler and vine.
Their muscles tense. One rises into a gallop, widening the field.

Its legs seize with strength and I remain in the space left behind:
the sudden nakedness of a northern forest. I am unable to follow—
The elk, in their way, have mastered living by mastering letting go.
Soon it will rain, and we will all wear our haloes of mist.

The Making of a Ghost

The *rap rap*

rap of ghosts at the door. Here are the steps
she must take when the great greats

cross yet another spilled eyelid of ocean water
and throng into the present tense.

This time the embarkment is holier than the last,
the locusts woven into maple trees

and the buzzards with luminous faces.
She gnashes open the green cardamom,

sheds the seeds into her own grave
and settles into equilibrium:

the meal of one story into another's mouth.
All of her meat another lineage,

an answering before the wound is born.
With sweet water from her language of rivers,

she washes her body three times.
This is what the ghosts pass down: one hand

over the other, a valley of long stems,
and the ritual of washing her body an odd number

of times before rest.
She is laying down the past like a row of knives.

She begins here, ends here, roots here
in the pine forest overlain with clay.

Country, again, she is knocking
on the glass of your windows. She is jotting

down the script of your prairies.
Country, at last, gift her a homecoming.

House of Prayer

I walk into the beads of thirty-three *alhamdulillahs,*
I walk into my childhood mouth, repeat *alhamdulillah.*

Four decades ago, father too walked into this prayer, his body nested
into the aeroplane, his *alhamdulillah*

humming deep until it matched the scale of the engine. It was during
that first crossing from one *alhamdulillah*

to another home, that my father crushed open the chasm he has since
passed down to every poem I write: [   ]

the hollow, the forgotten Qur'an lodged deep in the night of an
unopened drawer. My quest to belong. *Alhamdulillah,*

forgive me, forgive me. I praise once again, and symmetry like the
wings of a migrating bird, I repeat *alhamdulillah*

and rinse and repeat, rinse and repeat, like the *rokrok*
of an egret. I hold this *tasbih* to count my *alhamdulillahs*

thirty-three times, ninety-nine times: the key is to walk again and again
into the holy, repeating *alhamdulillah,*

alhamdulillah, alhamdullilah, until the skyward calm. Father, what did
you hope for when you uttered *alhamdulillah,*

when you rinsed over the Atlantic in that giant bird? When the egg
cracked open and the yolk of *alhamdullilah*

spilled onto a new coast? Was it travelling homeward
or away from homeland? I have learned that *alhamdulillah*

does not resemble a border, but is a house of its own.
Alhamdulillah glints beyond language: praise be to God.

My tongue holds the syllables, unhooks the praise
in my own last name: *h-m-d.* Always, I recite *alhamdulillah.*

On My Tongue

Bismillah is my first memory.

I became a bird in the Qur'an
at hardly eight years old.

I opened the dark green cover
and revealed the two

slippery hearts: Arabic
and its English translation.

On Saturdays, I learned to repeat
passages in Arabic,

to recite the Qur'an
in its truest language—

otherwise are the locusts
really locusts?

I read and read, and yet
struggled to recite in Arabic.

This was not a problem
with my memory.

I learned in a week how
to recite the first verse in English.

Sometimes I think every Qur'an
has a dark green cover.

Sometimes I think I still
become a bird

when, in my mind, I remember
Bismillah, ar-Rahman, ar-Rahim.

This must be the reason I
continue to love.

On my tongue, there is
a short-horned grasshopper.

Bismillah, I reach for you again.

Acknowledgements

To my family and my partner – all my love.

Warmest gratitude to the editors of the following magazines, who first took a chance on this work and published earlier versions of these poems: *The Adroit Journal, Tupelo Quarterly, Glass: A Journal of Poetry, Gulf Coast Magazine, The London Magazine, The /t3mz/ Review, The Paris Review Daily* and *Palette Poetry*.

In 2019, 'Love Poem with Elk and Punctuation' and 'Prairie Storm' won the CBC Literary Prize in Poetry. 'Hinge,' won the Gulf Coast Prize for Poetry.

'The Making of a Ghost' was recognized as part of the 92Y Discovery Poetry Contest. 'House of Prayer' was a runner-up for the Palette Poetry Prize.

Thank you to the Calgary Arts Development for their ongoing support of my practice.

Special thank you to my dear friends Nicole Lachat, Laura Schoenberg, and Jay G Ying for entering these imaginary worlds with me over the years. I am so lucky to be on this journey with you.

To my teachers, Bert Almon, Alan Gillis, Garrett Hongo, Shawna Lemay, and Derek Walcott, I am so grateful for your guidance, care, and generosity. And to my mentors, Mimi Khalvati and Eduardo C. Corral, thank you for believing in this work.

The epigraph for this pamphlet is from '7. Partition,' a section in the collection *Schizophrene* by Bhanu Kapil (Nightboat Books, 2011).

Thank you to the brilliant team at **ignition**press for the care you've shown my work.